The Night Sky

Written by Alice Pernick

Illustrated by Lisa Desimini

SCHOLASTIC INC.

New York Toronto London Auckland Sydney

Printed in the U.S.A.
ISBN 0-590-27385-X

7 8 9 10 09 00 99 98 97 96 95

When the sun sets at the end of the day, the night sky begins to twinkle and shine.

There are many things to see in the night sky.

The moon is the brightest light in the night sky. Sometimes the moon looks full and round.

Sometimes the moon looks thin and curved. It looks different at different times of the month.

Millions of stars twinkle in the night sky. Some look brighter than others. Some look blue and some look white.

Groups of stars that
form patterns in the sky
are called constellations.

Little Dipper
Big Dipper

Some of the brightest points of light in the night sky are planets. They look like stars, but they do not twinkle.

Look at the sky just before the sun rises. You might see Venus shining brightly in the east.

Venus

Comets blaze across the sky. They look like stars with long tails. Comets don't pass by often. If you see a comet, it's your lucky night!

Tips for Watching the Night Sky

Go out on a night when the moon is not bright.

Pick a spot where buildings and trees won't get in the way.

Close your eyes and get used to the dark.

Open your eyes and look up. What do you see?